MANAGING FOR COMMITMENT

Developing Loyalty In A Changing Workplace

Carol Kinsey Goman, Ph.D.

CRISP PUBLICATIONS, INC.
Los Altos, California

MANAGING FOR COMMITMENT
Developing Loyalty In A Changing Workplace

Carol Kinsey Goman, Ph.D.

CREDITS
Editor: **Tony Hicks**
Layout and Composition: **Interface Studio**
Cover Design: **Carol Harris**
Artwork: **Ralph Mapson**

Copyright © 1991 by Crisp Publications, Inc.
Printed in the United States of America

English language Crisp books are distributed worldwide. Our major international distributors include:

CANADA: Reid Publishing Ltd., Box 69559—109 Thomas St., Oakville, Ontario Canada L6J 7R4. TEL: (416) 842-4428, FAX: (416) 842-9327

AUSTRALIA: Career Builders, P. O. Box 1051, Springwood, Brisbane, Queensland, Australia 4127. TEL: 841-1061, FAX: 841-1580

NEW ZEALAND: Career Builders, P. O. Box 571, Manurewa, Auckland, New Zealand. TEL: 266-5276, FAX: 266-4152

JAPAN: Phoenix Associates Co., Mizuho Bldg. 2-12-2, Kami Osaki, Shinagawa-Ku, Tokyo 141, Japan. TEL: 3-443-7231, FAX: 3-443-7640

Selected Crisp titles are also available in other languages. Contact International Rights Manager Tim Polk at (415) 949-4888 for more information.

Library of Congress Catalog Card Number 90-84926
Goman, Carol Kinsey
ISBN 1-56052-099-X

PREFACE

The coming years will witness more change and complexity than our organizations have ever faced. To meet the challenge of a vacillating economy and global competition, we need to engage the creative energies of our work force. We need their commitment and loyalty. Yet the last decade has seen a weakening of the bonds of trust between management and workers.

The traditional views of commitment and loyalty no longer apply. Changes in the business world and in the work force require a different approach. Employees can no longer expect lifetime employment. Nor can they expect a promise of stability. Change has become a fact of corporate life.

On the other hand, today's workers are far more mobile than the previous generation, and they have a different set of values. Employees no longer believe that top management has a pre-determined plan for their career progression. Workers today are creating their own career paths, and many consider job hopping a normal route to professional success.

Opportunities abound for those managers who understand today's worker, and use this understanding to create realistic guidelines for mutual commitment.

The skills and strategies in this book will help you to:

- Understand your role in the changing workplace.

- Explore the changing values of today's employees.

- Realize the advantages of mutual commitment between management and workers.

- Manage people through change.

- Prepare subordinates for new roles and responsibilities.

- Become a values-driven manager.

- Revitalize your loyalty and commitment to yourself and to your organization.

This book will give you the step-by-step advice and activities to become a master at managing for commitment.

Good luck!

Carol Kinsey Goman

Carol Kinsey Goman, Ph.D.

ABOUT THIS BOOK

MANAGING FOR COMMITMENT is not like most books. It stands out in an important way. It's not a book to read—it's a book to *use*. The unique self-paced format of this book and the many worksheets encourage the reader to get involved and try some new ideas immediately.

This book will show you how to build trust and commitment into your management results. It presents simple, sound techniques that can make a dramatic change in your understanding and effectiveness in the workplace.

MANAGING FOR COMMITMENT (and the other titles listed in the back of this book) can be used effectively in a number of ways. Here are some possibilities:

Individual Study. Because the book is self-instructional, all that is needed is a quiet place, some time, and a pencil. By completing the activities and exercises, you'll receive not only valuable feedback but also practical steps for self-improvements.

Workshops and Seminars. The book is an ideal preparation for a workshop or seminar. With the basics in hand, the quality of participation will improve, and more time can be spend on concept extensions and applications. The book can be read before the workshop, or it can be distributed at the beginning of a session, and the participants invited to work through the contents.

Remote Location Training. Books can be sent to those not able to attend training sessions at their main office.

There are other possibilities that depend on the objectives, program, or ideas of the user. One thing for sure, even after it has been read, this book will be looked at—and thought about—again and again.

TABLE OF CONTENTS

GETTING THE MOST FROM THIS BOOK

The process of rebuilding trust and commitment within an organization is often confusing. Many companies discovered that, in trying to become leaner and more competitive, they jeopardized the emotional connection between workers and employers. Often management is frustrated by the lack of productivity among employees who don't seem to care anymore.

All of us are quite aware that the old-style, traditional loyalty is gone. But few of us know exactly what to expect in its place. This book will help managers understand the changes taking place in the business climate and within the hearts of the workforce. This book also presents strategies and skills for developing mutual respect and commitment.

Each company is unique and requires a specialized approach to insure positive outcomes. As a manager, you must customize and experiment. I encourage you to use questionnaires and focus groups to survey your subordinates and to tailor your management strategy according to the results. I invite you to use this book as a guide, along with your own common sense, good judgment, and business experience.

ABOUT THE AUTHOR

Author, keynote speaker and seminar presenter, Carol Kinsey Goman is a nationally recognized authority on developing employee loyalty and commitment. She addresses conferences and conventions in the United States and Canada. Her workshops have been implemented at major corporations all across the country. They have helped thousands of managers and employees learn the skills they need to be successful in a changing work environment.

For more information on how you can use the *Managing for Commitment* seminar to help your organization, please call:

Carol Kinsey Goman, Ph.D.
Kinsey Consulting Services
P.O. Box 8255
Berkeley, CA 94707
(415) 943-7850

P A R T

I

The Changing Work Force

To make a living is no longer enough. Work also has to make a life.

—Peter Drucker, *Management*

MEET THE NEW WORK FORCE

Are you ready for the work force of the future? Recent studies show that in the United States, by the year 2000:

- Four out of five new members of the work force will be women, minorities, or immigrants.

- Two-thirds of the new entrants to the work force will be female.

- Immigrants are projected to account for more than 23% of the additions to the work force.

- White males will comprise only 15% of additions to the work force.

- College graduates will likely average 10 (or more) jobs before retiring.

- People will change careers every 10 years.

- 40% of employees believe they have a fundamental right to self-fulfillment from their work.

- Singles may constitute the majority of households. They will want work that gives them meaning and engages their emotions along with their minds.

- Approximately 76 million baby boomers are in their forties, yearning for upward mobility and career challenges.

- There is a growing shortage of entry-level workers. In 1985, 16- to 24-year-olds comprised 30% of the labor pool. By 2000, that percentage will drop to 16%.

- The average age of the work force will rise to 40 years.

- The percentage of dual-income couples will increase to 57%.

- 41% of new jobs will be high-skill jobs, yet many new workers will lack even basic skills.

- A general acceptance of diversity among people is growing as an explicit value.

A survey by the Public Agenda Foundation finds that fewer than one out of four employees (23%) say they work at full potential.

Management author Peter Drucker says we need to boost productivity by 50% over the next 10 years without adding numbers to the work force.

Key Question: How can management boost productivity from the new work force?

Solution: FIND OUT WHAT WORKERS WANT AND GIVE IT TO THEM!

WORKING WITH THE NEW WORK FORCE

Today's work force is diverse—women, minorities, and immigrants are bringing their own special issues and talents to our organizations. Their diverse personal needs cannot be met by the work ethic of the industrial age. With an expanded variety (but dwindling number) of entry-level employees, management will need more understanding and flexibility.

Female workers bring with them their relationship values and nurturing skills. They will want to express these values and use these skills in the workplace. Three-fifths of all women over age 16 will hold paying jobs in the year 2000. Yet most employment policies concerning pay and benefits were designed when men worked and women stayed home.

The number of young people is shrinking, the pace of industrial change is increasing, and skill requirements are rising. So the task of fully utilizing minorities is urgent. But minorities and immigrants have ethnic and cultural concerns different from those of white males, for whom most organizational policies were created. We need to reexamine current policies in view of today's realities.

More workers today have young or elderly dependents. This added responsibility is especially hard on single-parent families and families in which both parents work. Organizations need to address the sometimes conflicting needs of these working parents. For example, schedules or work locations may need to be altered to balance work and family demands, and more companies need to include child or elder care in their benefits packages.

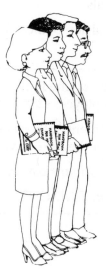

Work life today brings pressure and stress. Employees are asked to do more with less, and many struggle with a feeling of overload. Uncertain about their futures, many workers keep a low profile and constantly look over their shoulder. This is undesirable, particularly at a time when we need to encourage risk taking and creativity. Responding to on-the-job stress begins with acknowledging the realities of the situation and then helping people find ways to cope.

Twenty years ago not even 5% of the population expected to develop their potential and find satisfaction through work. Today 40% of employees believe they have a right to self-fulfillment, self-expression, and personal growth. They want to find meaningful jobs and work for organizations that are making worthwhile contributions to the world. A study conducted by the Stanford Research Institute predicted that the percentage of such "inner directed" workers would increase during this decade.

Educated, salaried professionals—sometimes called gold-collar workers—are increasingly valued by organizations. These highly skilled employees expect to work hard and put in long hours in return for top salaries and benefits. They also expect promotions and career-building opportunities. Motivating, developing, and retaining these prize workers is essential for any organization. Helping people develop as top-level professionals means spending money on education, training, cross-training, and retraining.

Members of the baby-boom generation are beginning to enter their forties. They are also entering the corporate boardrooms. Their values are already influencing corporate values and philosophy with New Age thinking.

Skilled members of the baby-bust generation (entry-level applicants aged 16 to 24 years old, whose numbers are decreasing) are disturbing company routine with their demands for quality of life. To many baby-busters, work is just one segment of a whole life filled with many interests—including more time allotted for a personal agenda. Working with the younger generation of employees calls for management finesse and tolerance.

For all their differences, though, members of the new work force agree on one thing. They feel best about themselves and their work when they are emotionally committed to the company they work for. They see commitment as a high priority.

HOW HAVE YOU ADJUSTED?

Every industry and every location has its own challenges when coping with the new work force. What have you found to be true in your company? Write your answers in the spaces provided.

How has the work force changed in your organization?

_____

_____

_____

_____

_____

_____

_____

How has the organization changed in response to the new work force?

_____

_____

_____

_____

_____

_____

_____

How has your management style changed in response to the new work force?

_____

_____

_____

_____

_____

_____

_____

P A R T

II

The Need For Commitment

Modern companies should be communities, not battlefields.
At their heart lie covenants between executives and employees
that rest on shared commitment to ideas, to issues, to values,
to goals, and to management processes.
                    —Max De Pree, chairman of Herman Miller, Inc.

COMMITMENT CHECKLIST

Commitment plays an important part in achieving a high level of performance in any endeavor. To check your views on commitment, read the following statements and indicate whether you think they are true or false.

TRUE   FALSE

_____ _____ 1. It is important to create an environment in which employees can meet their needs while meeting the needs of the organization.

_____ _____ 2. Commitment to the organization is improved when employees are recognized for their contributions.

_____ _____ 3. The mission of an organization can inspire commitment.

_____ _____ 4. The level of employee commitment has little to do with management's communication practices.

_____ _____ 5. Commitment generally stays the same whether or not employees participate in planning projects.

_____ _____ 6. Most employees prefer to work where they can feel loyal and committed to their employers.

_____ _____ 7. Managers can do little to elevate employee commitment.

_____ _____ 8. Productivity generally increases when commitment increases.

The answers to 1, 2, 3, 6, and 8 are TRUE

NEW RULES OF THE GAME

A few years ago every career move was supposed to be upward. Promotions came regularly. Success meant job security all the way to retirement. Personal feelings were secondary to corporate harmony. The work week was 40 hours, with evenings and weekends for family.

Today, success has been redefined by both the organization and its workers. Guaranteed lifetime employment is a thing of the past. A company can no longer guarantee even a specific job for an employee. If a person wants to remain with an organization, he or she must expect to upgrade skills continuously and master several jobs and functions.

Corporate pyramids have flattened through restructurings. Employees remain at one job level longer. They may go years between promotions, regardless of their quality of work. Lateral moves are becoming routine, and even desirable. People struggle to balance lives overflowing with competing priorities.

Success for today's new employees includes inner fulfillment—independence, control, challenge. Personal satisfaction and flexibility are becoming top-ranked career goals. People want to feel that their efforts matter and their work makes a contribution.

Success also means compensation. A good pay package includes desirable benefits and/or an equity stake or profit sharing. Job hopping—even career hopping—is more and more of an option.

In all of these changes, what happened to company loyalty and worker commitment? Did it die or just change forms? How does an organization benefit from increased employee commitment? Why are employees now saying that loyalty is more important to them than ever before? What management skills are most needed to bridge the trust gap between employers and employees? And how can an understanding of this issue make you even more valuable to your organization?

These are questions this book addresses. Ahead, you find information, examples, and exercises designed to develop your ability to manage for commitment.

YOUR IDEAS ABOUT COMMITMENT

1. In the space provided, write what the word *commitment* means to you.

_____

_____

_____

_____

2. Recall a time when your commitment to work was high. What were the details?

_____

_____

_____

_____

3. Recall a time when your commitment to work was low. What were the details?

_____

_____

_____

_____

4. What were the main differences in management practices or organizational cultures between situations 2 and 3?

_____

_____

_____

YOUR IDEAS ABOUT COMMITMENT
(Continued)

5. Is it important to you personally to feel loyalty and commitment to your managers and organization? Why?

_____

_____

_____

_____

6. Is it important to you as a manager to have subordinates who are loyal and committed to you and the organization? Why?

_____

_____

_____

_____

7. What does your organization do to build employee commitment?

_____

_____

_____

_____

8. What management practices do you use to develop commitment in your employees?

_____

_____

_____

_____

THE BENEFITS OF HIGH COMMITMENT

When employee commitment is high, management benefits in many ways, including:

> **High Quality.** Committed employees care about the quality of the goods or services that the company provides. They are eager to offer creative ideas on how to improve products or systems. And organizations that stand for quality and service are more likely to attract talented workers who are looking to commit to a company they can be proud of.

> **High Performance.** Employees with high commitment to the organization care about corporate goals and objectives. They are more willing to put out the extra effort necessary to increase performance and production.

> **Low Turnover.** When employees are committed to the organization and feel that the organization is committed to them, they are less likely to quit their jobs. Turnover and absenteeism drop substantially. In fact, committed employees value their existing work relationships so highly that they may even pass over more lucrative opportunities.

> **Good Reputation.** Workers who are committed to the organization speak well of it to their friends and in the community. This goes a long way to enhance the company's reputation with other employees, customers, and potential employees.

> **High Morale.** Committed employees are happy in their work. They love their jobs. When employee morale is high, there is less illness, fewer accidents, more fun, and a heightened atmosphere of general goodwill.

> **Team Spirit.** When employees are committed to the highest objectives of the organization, there is more cooperation and group interaction. Teams work together readily as they bond with one another. Team spirit comes naturally when people are committed to the organization and to their co-workers.

> **Ability to Attract Employees.** Almost everyone wants to work in the kind of company just described. They want to bond with their co-workers, love their jobs, and feel committed to their organization. Organizations that understand this need will tend to attract the most talented people from a dwindling pool of well-skilled workers.

THE HIGH COST OF LOW COMMITMENT

When employee commitment is low, management may see some of the following consequences:

> **Low Quality.** As commitment drops, so does employee concern about the quality of goods or services put out by the company. As risk-averse employees hold back their suggestions for needed improvements, quality is sure to suffer.

> **Low Performance.** Employees with low commitment are satisfied to do the minimum—just enough to keep their jobs. The goals of the organization seem remote and unattached to them in any meaningful way.

> **High Turnover.** Without commitment, employees may simply leave the organization at the first sign of trouble or discord.

> **Poor Reputation.** Companies may spend millions of dollars building a corporate reputation, only to see it destroyed by badmouthing from disgruntled employees.

> **Low Morale.** When commitment slides, employees no longer look forward to coming to work. They fall victim to stress-related illnesses, and on-the-job accidents increase. If people feel oppressed or unappreciated, the general atmosphere of the workplace will suffer.

> **Low Team Spirit.** Workers with low commitment have an attitude of ''every person for themselves.'' Obsessed with guarding their own special interests or turf, employees withdraw from productive interaction with one another. They feel disenfranchised from the organization and from each other.

> **Inability to Attract Employees.** Since commitment is so important to most people, potential employees will look for organizations that build trust and loyalty. Organizations that do not understand and respond to this employee need will lose out in the competition for talented workers.

THE GREAT BALANCING ACT

Today's workers are trying to balance many aspects of a full and varied life. They sometimes feel torn between equally important commitments. When people are forced to choose between the things they value, they often become unhappy and stressed.

At work, employees may feel a strong commitment to their boss, their co-workers, the union, or the customer. Commitments to their careers, to professional standards, and to the goals of the organization all vie for attention. Outside work, family and personal interests are gaining importance as employees reassess the full meaning of success. Employees should not be made to feel disloyal to the organization just because they are also loyal to personal goals. The effective manager discovers what employees are committed to—and then fits organizational commitment into that pattern. In this way, being committed to the organizaton is seen as supporting, not competing with, other important commitments.

For example, one manager spoke of an employee who was extremely committed to improving the environment. Luckily, the organization was also sensitive to environmental issues. The employee was encouraged to work on a company-wide recycling task force. When it was understood that serving the goals of the organization was also serving the environment, the employee developed a set of loyalties that strengthened one another.

The first step is to have your work team complete the exercise on the next page. After each team member has clarified his or her commitments, you can lead a discussion about the ways in which commitments can compete with or strengthen one another. Ask for examples and share creative ideas from the group.

MULTIPLE COMMITMENTS EXERCISE AHEAD

MULTIPLE COMMITMENTS EXERCISE

People have many commitments and priorities in their lives. What are the important commitments of your team? Make a copy of this form and invite each person in your work group to complete this exercise. Rate each commitment by circling a number from 1 ("least important") to 5 ("most important").

Commitment	Least Important				Most Important
Organization	1	2	3	4	5
Career	1	2	3	4	5
Personal ethics	1	2	3	4	5
Family	1	2	3	4	5
Significant other	1	2	3	4	5
Work group	1	2	3	4	5
Manager	1	2	3	4	5
Environment	1	2	3	4	5
Country	1	2	3	4	5
Friends	1	2	3	4	5
Customer	1	2	3	4	5
Subordinates	1	2	3	4	5
Health and wellness	1	2	3	4	5
Leisure time	1	2	3	4	5
Union	1	2	3	4	5
Department	1	2	3	4	5
Religion	1	2	3	4	5
Other _____	1	2	3	4	5

COMMITMENT TO SELF

Today's employees' first commitment is to themselves. Managers who accept this as part of human nature will look for ways in which commitment to self is strengthened by commitment to the organization.

People want to find meaning in their work. They also want their jobs to be an extension of their personal values and beliefs. If we could all join organizations whose values genuinely reflected our own, there would be an immediate increase in productivity, quality, and innovation across America.

Creating such a values match is both the employees' and management's responsibility. Employees need to have a clearer idea of what their personal philosophy and mission is, and management needs to communicate organizational culture and philosophy to help employees choose companies that match their own deeply held beliefs.

You can help your team members develop a strong sense of their own values. You may wish to work with an outside consultant who specializes in these kinds of programs, or you may personally conduct an interactive session. (Off-site locations are preferred for such sessions.)

The next exercise is a good basis for an interactive discussion. When individuals have created their own missions, you can lead an evaluation of the organization's mission and the ways in which it reflects team members' values. In this way, you will help people interlock multiple commitments.

INTERLOCKING MISSION EXERCISE AHEAD

INTERLOCKING MISSIONS EXERCISE

Employee Mission

Have your team members work on the following exercise individually, then compare answers.

Ask yourself the following questions, and write your answers in the spaces provided.

1. What do I stand for? (How would I like to be remembered?)

_____

_____

_____

2. What activities have provided me with the most enjoyment?

_____

_____

_____

3. What are my deepest personal values? (What do I strongly believe in?)

_____

_____

_____

4. How do I view my responsibilities to the community, to the country, to the world? (What social issues are the most important to me?)

_____

_____

_____

5. How do I want my job to make a difference? (Where does work fit into fulfilling my personal mission?)

_____

_____

_____

Organization Mission

Ask each member of the team to write his or her answers to the following questions. Then lead a discussion about the answers.

1. What is the organization's mission?

_____

_____

_____

2. What is the organization's view of its responsibilities to the community, the country, the world?

_____

_____

_____

3. What are the deepest values of the organization?

_____

_____

_____

4. What opportunities does the organization provide for helping each of us fulfill our personal missions?

_____

_____

_____

PART

III

Rebuilding Trust In The Workplace

The essence of business as it moves into the 21st century is going to be tapping the talent of good people. It's not how you locate the plants, it's how you locate the best people and motivate them. How you trust them and have them trust you.
—Reuben Mark, CEO of Colgate-Palmolive

LEVELS OF TRUST

A study conducted for the Life Insurance Agency Management Association concluded that the main difference between low-performance groups and high-performance groups was the degree to which employees said they trusted their immediate supervisors.

Trust in a relationship is a fragile thing. It doesn't come quickly—we tend to withhold trust until others prove themselves worthy of it—and yet it can be destroyed by one simple violation.

In their book *The Equity Factor*, Richard Huseman and John Hatfield describe attitudes and behaviors at different levels of trust:

1. HIGH TRUST
   When a high level of trust exists, people show little concern about getting their share from the relationship, because they know that the other party will not take advantage of them.

2. LOW TRUST
   People in low-trust relationships are preoccupied with seeing that they get their fair share and that the other party gets no more than a fair share.

3. NO TRUST
   People who have lost all trust in a situation live by the motto, "I'm going to get them before they get me. Who knows when they'll try to take advantage of me next?"

WHO DO YOU TRUST?

The two following surveys on page 25 and 26 present a series of descriptive statements.

Rate each statement on a scale of 1 (''almost never true'') to 4 (''almost always true''). Once you've written in your assessments of all the statements, add up the scores.

Take the first survey and then compare your trust level with those of managers interviewed by the author in a national study.

In the second survey, answer as you think your employees would. Then make copies for your entire work team. Ask them to answer anonymously and return the survey to you. Comparing your idea of their responses with their answers will give you valuable information about the level of trust in your organization.

Keep in mind that these surveys were originally created as part of a longer questionnaire developed for use in large-scale projects. They offer insight into general feelings, not exact measurements of trust levels.

FIRST SURVEY—MANAGERS

Rate each statement according to the following scale:

4 Almost always true
3 True most of the time
2 Seldom true
1 Almost never true

_____ When subordinates use their best judgment, they can be trusted to make good decisions.

_____ My subordinates care about their jobs and this organization.

_____ Most employees are basically honest and trustworthy.

_____ I will back up my employees if I think they are right, even if it jeopardizes my own job.

_____ My employees are talented and creative.

_____ Each of my subordinates knows more about his or her job than I do.

_____ My employees want to do a good job.

_____ My subordinates are involved in all important decisions concerning the individual or the department.

_____ My main job function is to create an environment in which people motivate and direct themselves toward a common goal.

_____ My employees are loyal to me and to this organization.

_____ **TOTAL SCORE**

(Compare your responses with information in the box below)

Evaluation

Here's what your score indicates:

10-20 There is a low level of trust between you and your subordinates.

21-25 Your trust level could use improvement.

26-35 This score indicates an adequate amount of trust in your working relationships with subordinates.

36-40 You have a strong trust relationship with your subordinates.

SECOND SURVEY—SUBORDINATES

Rate each statement according to the following scale:

> **4** Almost always true
> **3** True most of the time
> **2** Seldom true
> **1** Almost never true

_____ I understand my manager's management style.

_____ I feel free to take risks.

_____ I know that my manager will keep his or her word.

_____ I know that my manager trusts, respects, and appreciates me.

_____ My manager gives me timely and accurate information about the direction of this company and my role in it.

_____ I believe that my manager has the skills and knowledge required for the job.

_____ If I think my boss is right, I will back him or her up even if it means jeopardizing my own job.

_____ I am comfortable sharing personal feelings or concerns with my boss.

_____ I tend to be truthful and honest in my communications with my manager.

_____ My boss is committed to my growth and success.

_____ **TOTAL SCORE**

(Compare your responses with information in the box below)

Evaluation

Here's what your score indicates:

10-20   You have a low level of trust from your subordinates.

21-25   There is some lack of trust from your employees.

26-35   This score indicates that your employees generally trust you.

36-40   Your subordinates have a strong trust relationship with you.

NONDEPENDENT TRUST

As an individual and as a professional, you must care for yourself. Nondependent trust is not a selfish disregard for the goals of your organization or callous treatment of subordinates to get what you want. It simply reflects the understanding that your first loyalty is to yourself. Once you can clearly state your core values and career objectives, you can better align with people and organizations whose purposes support your own. In these affiliations, helping the company reach its objectives also serves your own agenda. Commitment to the organization then becomes an important part of commitment to yourself.

Developing nondependent trust in your business relationships requires a clear understanding of the responsibilities and rights of both parties—employees and management. Following are some thoughts on the subject. Look them over and then create your own. Better yet, make this a team effort with your work group.

Employee Responsibilities

1. As an employee, you take responsibility for yourself and your future. You are (in effect) ''self-employed.'' It is up to you to design and control your career.

2. You create a clear view of what you want your future to be.

3. You develop a plan and a strategy to attain your goals.

4. You realistically evaluate your skills and talents and plan for further personal growth.

5. You nurture a powerful belief in your ability to attain your goals.

Management Responsibilities

1. As a manager, you give employees a realistic overview of their rights and responsibilities in today's work environment.

2. You encourage employees to set goals and develop career strategies.

3. You expect that people's first loyalty will be personal. Therefore, you show employees how being loyal to the organization can also serve their own objectives.

4. You help others align with your organization by clearly presenting the corporate values, philosophy, and mission.

5. You offer employees education and training in skills that will prepare them for the future.

28

NONDEPENDENT TRUST (Continued)

Employee Rights

1. Employees have a right to be treated with courtesy and respect.

2. They have a right to honest and timely evaluations.

3. They have a right to know the objectives and future plans of their company.

4. They have a right to know how their efforts contribute to the success of the organization.

5. They have a right to question management decisions.

6. They have a right to expect management to care about their well-being, health, and safety.

7. They have a right to make mistakes.

Management Rights

1. Management has a right to be treated with courtesy and respect.

2. It has a right to expect honesty and trustworthy behavior from employees.

3. It has a right to expect employees to express creative ideas for improving the job or the organization.

4. It has a right to expect employees to care about the success of the organization.

5. It has a right to make mistakes.

RESPONSIBILITIES

Now it's time for your work group to make its own lists. Let this exercise be the foundation for the process of developing nondependent trust in your organization.

Write your lists in the spaces provided.

Employee Responsibilities

1. _____
   _____

2. _____
   _____

3. _____
   _____

4. _____
   _____

5. _____
   _____

Management Responsibilities

1. _____
   _____

2. _____
   _____

3. _____
   _____

4. _____
   _____

5. _____
   _____

RIGHTS

Write your lists in the spaces provided.

Employee Rights

1. _____

   _____

2. _____

   _____

3. _____

   _____

4. _____

   _____

5. _____

   _____

Management Rights

1. _____

   _____

2. _____

   _____

3. _____

   _____

4. _____

   _____

5. _____

   _____

P A R T

IV

Maintaining Commitment

This is a little book for those who intend to survive—for managers prepared to initiate drastic change. It is about every company faced with the need to rethink its goals and restructure itself.

—Alvin Toffler, *The Adaptive Corporation*

MANAGING CHANGE

No one knows who first said ''change is the only constant,'' but those words are certainly true. Change is the most pervasive influence in today's workplace. And the pace of organizational change is increasing.

Because of the dangers and uncertainty inherent in change, many managers become frightened when facing it. Some resist change because they fear a loss of control. Others impose massive changes on their organizations, seemingly oblivious to the impact on those involved. Both the ''resistant'' and the ''ramrod'' management styles make it almost impossible for employees to cope successfully with change.

"RESISTANTS"   "RAMROD"

By contrast, a growing number of managers are learning to control change by becoming more creative* and resilient. They use management strategies that maximize the advantages in change for their subordinates, and they advance change effectively for themselves and their organizations. To manage change successfully they address three key areas: preparation, communication, and participation.

Creativity In Business, also by Carol Kinsey Goman, is an excellent source of instruction and inspiration for developing your creative ability and applying it on the job. To order it, use the list in the back of this book.

PREPARATION

> A consultant to a Fortune 500 company said:
>
> *I was brought in to oversee the implementation of a major restructuring in an international organization. I discovered that the top 1,000 people were totally confused about the direction of the change and the reasons for it.*
>
> A middle manager at a midsized service company said:
>
> *Nobody thought the whole thing out before it was announced. It felt like the business was going down the drain and* they *were just trying anything.*

Statements like the above reflect the potentially confusing and capricious nature of change. Strategic preparation requires managers to think through the human implications *before* announcing a major change. By doing this, you will have the opportunity to take the following steps.

Check the steps that are important to you.

_____ To understand the change better.

_____ To approach the change from the point of view of my employees.

_____ To prepare for resistance.

_____ To begin to develop a working strategy for implementing the change.

_____ To have a framework for asking my boss questions about the change.

_____ To position the change from the perspective of the organization's mission and goals.

_____ To build support for the change.

_____ To predetermine the stumbling blocks that might prevent the change.

_____ To discover the consequences of not changing.

_____ To assess my own reaction to the change.

CHANGE PREPARATION CHECKLIST

From the very beginning of the change, managers need to consider how it will affect employees and their daily work life. Here are some areas you could begin with. Ask yourself the following questions, and write your answers in the spaces provided.

Who will be affected by this change?

_____

_____

_____

Who will help implement or administer this change?

_____

_____

_____

Who else needs to be consulted?

_____

_____

_____

What new skills and behaviors will be required?

_____

_____

_____

How will the new skills and behaviors be taught and rewarded?

_____

_____

_____

Does the change necessitate new policies and procedures?

_____

_____

_____

CHANGE PREPARATION CHECKLIST
(Continued)

In what ways does the change support the mission of the organization?

_____

_____

_____

How does the change affect the duties and responsibilities of those who report to me?

_____

_____

_____

How does the change affect my duties and responsibilities?

_____

_____

_____

What are the advantages of the change to my employees? How might these be expanded or enhanced?

_____

_____

_____

What are the disadvantages? How might these be reduced?

_____

_____

_____

Exactly what is the reason for this change?

_____

_____

_____

What are the penalties to the organization and its employees for not changing?

_____

_____

_____

Who will most likely resist the change? Why? How can I minimize the resistance?

_____

_____

_____

When does the change go into effect?

_____

_____

_____

How will the change be evaluated?

_____

_____

_____

Who supports the change? Are the supporters respected?

_____

_____

_____

Who has gone through a similar change and with what results?

_____

_____

_____

How will the change be introduced and by whom?

_____

_____

_____

Why do I personally resist or support the change?

_____

_____

_____

COMMUNICATION

Effective change depends on continuous communications. In many cases, the manner in which change is presented is far more important than the change itself. Commitment-building managers are effective communicators. By and large they use the following methods in communicating change.

- **They communicate change in advance whenever possible.**
  Any abrupt change or surprise is harder to accept. To reduce fears of the unknown and squelch the fantasies of the rumor mill, you need to inform your employees up front. The more people understand about the situation, the more likely they are to buy in to the need for change. It is especially helpful to explore how the change will affect the organizational structure, job descriptions, employee compensation, and training. Doing so allows people to make enlightened choices about their futures.

- **They don't sugar-coat negativity—they make sense of it.**
  The most effective managers today are those the work force trusts to "tell it like it is." Candid communication of change demands that both positive and negative consequences be openly weighed. Even an unpopular decision is more easily accepted when it makes good sense.

- **They show a genuine concern for individuals.**
  In various surveys, employees report that the best bosses are empathetic and directly address personal concerns. A manager in a major company routinely asks his peers what it is that they manage. The answers he gets are those you might expect—"the marketing department," "the front-office staff," and so on. His reply is: "That's interesting. I manage weddings, divorces, lovers' quarrels, and deaths in the family...all human conditions."

Empathetic managers help people adapt to change. They present it from the perspective of those affected. They point out the benefits and the ways in which the change will help people capitalize on strengths. They look for ways to make change a win-win situation for the organization and the individual, so that changing together is profitable and fulfilling for both.

- **They have good listening skills.**
  Communication is a two-way street. It is just as important to listen as to speak. People give you verbal and nonverbal information every time you meet. Some managers have learned to take the time to listen attentively to their employees. They ask open-ended questions to draw people out, and they pay close attention to what is said. They make eye contact with the person speaking and show genuine interest. They make sure they've understood what was said by staying aware not only of the words but also of language and the emotions behind the words. They check their accuracy by paraphrasing key points and repeating them to the speaker.

- **They know the strengths and weaknesses of their communication style.**
  Your style of communicating directly influences your interactions with others. The more you learn about the ways in which you and your team communicate, the more effectively you can address individuals. Obviously, the reverse is also true: the more your employees learn about your style, the easier it will be for them to approach you in effective ways. Following is a short exercise to give you an indication of your primary communication style.

WHAT'S YOUR COMMUNICATION STYLE?

Consider the following statements. In the space provided, check (✔) the answer that best fits you.

1. **I am most likely to impress others as:**

   ____ **(a)** abrupt and to the point.

   ____ **(b)** caring and idealistic.

   ____ **(c)** logical and analytical.

   ____ **(d)** intellectual and complex.

   ____ **(e)** open-minded and adaptable.

2. **When I work on a project, I am most successful with:**

   ____ **(a)** a hands-on approach.

   ____ **(b)** an interactive group effort.

   ____ **(c)** a good system in place.

   ____ **(d)** far-out speculation.

   ____ **(e)** trying anything that looks possible.

3. **When I think about a job problem, I:**

   ____ **(a)** concentrate on the things I can see, hear, and touch.

   ____ **(b)** concentrate on the people involved.

   ____ **(c)** analyze what preceded it and what I plan next.

   ____ **(d)** think about concepts and the relationship between events.

   ____ **(e)** want to go into action quickly.

4. **When confronted by others with a different point of view, I can usually make progress by:**

   ____ **(a)** bringing in an expert.

   ____ **(b)** trying to put myself in others' shoes.

   ____ **(c)** helping others to see things calmly and logically.

   ____ **(d)** relying on my ability to pull ideas together.

   ____ **(e)** negotiating well.

5. **In communicating with others, I most value:**

   _____ **(a)** information based on people's experience.

   _____ **(b)** information based on people's feelings.

   _____ **(c)** information based on statistics and data.

   _____ **(d)** information from a great variety of sources.

   _____ **(e)** information that stresses the immediate payoff.

6. **In communicating with others, I tend to ignore:**

   _____ **(a)** information from people who haven't had direct experience.

   _____ **(b)** information with too many graphs and statistics.

   _____ **(c)** information that is more emotional than logical.

   _____ **(d)** information that seems one-sided and prematurely decided.

   _____ **(e)** information that focuses too much on long-term benefits.

Analysis of Answers

To obtain an approximate indication of your primary communication style,* enter below the number of times you selected answers in each category:

(a) _____ Realist

(b) _____ Idealist

(c) _____ Analyst

(d) _____ Synthesist

(e) _____ Pragmatist

---

*These categories represent different styles of thinking as defined by the InQ questionnaire by Bramson-Parlette. For information on ''Styles of Thinking''—a team-building seminar—contact Carol Kinsey Goman at Kinsey Consulting Services, P.O. Box 8255, Berkeley, CA 94709; (415) 943-7850.

PRIMARY COMMUNICATION STYLES

REALISTS hold an empirical world view. Facts, to a realist, are whatever can be seen, heard, or felt. Realists tend to be action oriented and are often found in production as trouble-shooters and in high-pressure job situations. They are hands-on problem solvers. As communicators, they tend to value input from experts—people who have been successful in similar situations.

IDEALISTS value and foster relationships. They prefer to approach problems by coming to consensus agreement. They seek solutions that will best serve all concerned. By nature, idealists are visionaries with high standards. As communicators, they project caring and concern for others, but they also hold high expectations for quality and performance. Idealists are most interested in the long-term benefits for society.

ANALYSTS are logical, straight-line thinkers. If it isn't rational, it isn't real. Accurate and thorough, analysts are gifted at reasoning and deductive logic. Most engineers are analysts. They rely on systems and formulas that will remain valid over time. As communicators, they value data and logical presentations.

SYNTHESISTS are fascinated with opposing ideas and positions. They have developed a special kind of curiosity and creativity that approaches problems with an attitude of ''what if...'' and ''on the other hand....'' They excel in coming up with original ideas. There is a high percentage of synthesists in the scientific community. As communicators, synthesists value multiple inputs from a variety of sources.

PRAGMATISTS tolerate change and ambiguity better than most people. They have little vested in "the right way" of doing things, because to a pragmatist, all solutions might possibly be right. Resourceful and expedient, they are good marketers. As communicators, pragmatists value solutions that take one step at a time and lead to payoff in the near future.

No one communication style is good or bad. Any style can be used effectively—just as any can be taken to excess. Realists need not be so abrupt that they seem to be uncaring. Idealists need not try too hard to find solutions that will please everyone and wind up pleasing no one. Analysts need not place too much faith in a formula that is no longer appropriate in a changing reality. Synthesists need not spend so much time playing with ideas that they never come to a conclusion. And pragmatists need not value expediency so much that they end up being shortsighted and shallow.

When communicating for commitment, the important thing is to recognize that different people have different styles and to be sensitive to these differences. When your team members understand each other's communication styles, group commitment and problem-solving skills are enhanced.

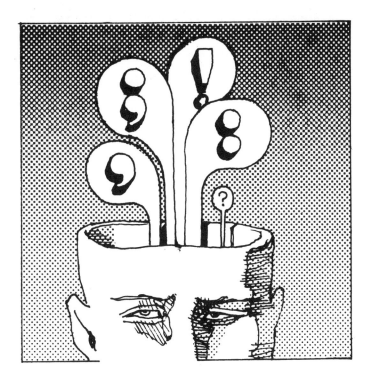

PARTICIPATION

Will Rogers once said, "We are all ignorant, just on different subjects." The managers who successfully bring their employees through traumatic change are the ones who surround themselves with people whose abilities complement their own. To these managers, change is a participative process. The most effective managers understand that

> Every worker knows his or her job best.

and

> The sum of ideas and commitment from the entire work force
> is greater than any solo effort by a manager.

Managers of change are catalysts, creating synergy in their work force. To harness creative commitment, managers delegate responsibility and authority. They utilize formal and informal groups to design and implement change. They encourage subordinates to think ahead and approach change proactively. They promote ownership by involving people, valuing their input, and acting on suggestions.

The managers who are most adept at managing the change process agree with the chief executive officer who said: "Your success at managing change depends solely on your ability to communicate and to get people involved."

THE HUMAN SIDE OF CHANGE

People tend to go through predictable phases in reaction to change: denial, resistance, exploration, and finally commitment. Effective leadership can facilitate the process of moving a group through the phases from denial to commitment, even in times of complete organizational restructuring and reorganization.

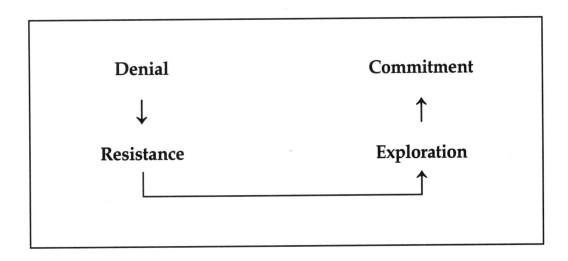

Understanding the impact on people at each phase will help you design change-management strategies that build commitment. Since organizational change is a continuing condition, change-management skills are increasingly important. The challenge is learning to move people through all transitions as smoothly and creatively as possible. A key component is letting people know what they can expect and how to respond to the challenges presented.*

---

*The information in this section is adapted from *Managing Organizational Change* by Cynthia Scott and Dennis Jaffe. For order information, see the back of this book.

DENIAL

Many employees' first response to an announcement of an organizational restructuring will be denial. "It will never happen to this company...or if it does, it won't affect me." This is a typical reaction not only of individuals, but also of entire departments, companies, and even communities. In one of my seminars, a participant reported that people in his community still talk about the mines reopening. The townspeople haven't yet faced the fact that the mines are closed—although they've been closed for 20 years.

At the denial stage of the cycle, employees need continuous information about the restructuring process. They want to know:

Who is staying?

How will they be informed?

Who is leaving?

How will they be informed?

How will the departing employees be treated?

What will happen to the people who remain?

Why is this happening?

What else is changing?

What will stay the same?

What will the restructured organization be like?

How soon is this happening?

Exactly how will it affect me?

Employees going through denial about a major change within their companies feel numb. The announcement doesn't seem to sink in. This stage can be prolonged if employees are not encouraged to register their reaction or if management expects the employees to move directly into the new ways. Denial is harmful because it impedes the natural progression of healing, by which we move forward from a loss (in this case, loss of the old way of doing things). Employees who stay in denial stay focused on the way things were, instead of exploring how they can or need to change.

On the other hand, when employees are supported through this phase, when they are encouraged to understand and face reality, then even a total restructuring can bring opportunities for personal and professional growth.

Diagnosing Denial

It is common to observe withdrawal; focusing on the past; there is activity but not much gets done.

Managing Denial

Confront individuals with information. Let them know that the change will happen. Explain what to expect and suggest actions they can take to adjust to the change. Give them time to let things sink in; then schedule a planning session to talk things over.

RESISTANCE

Resistance occurs when people have moved through the numbness of denial and begin to experience self-doubt, frustration, fear, or uncertainty because of the change. When a company is sold or merged or lays off workers, employees go through a stage of grieving. Elizabeth Kubler-Ross identified this stage in conjunction with her work with the dying. Losing one's expectations, hopes, and beliefs can be like going through a kind of death for certain employees. Employees grieving over the personal impact of a change, or resentful over the laying off of their colleagues, may find it hard to get down to business as usual. Productivity may dip drastically, and accidents, illness, and work-related absences may multiply.

When it is made difficult for employees to express their feelings openly, things get worse. Anxiety runs high, mistakes are made, deadlines are missed. Work often grinds to a standstill for weeks. One employee who lost his job after 17 years' employment said, ''People see a company slowly disintegrating. They keep their heads down and become part of the furniture.''

Management can assist workers through this difficult time by creating opportunities for people to express their feelings. This often requires the skill and guidance of special counselors, but there are many things that you as a manager can do.

You can help people to progress through the resistance phase, first of all by preparing them for it. As a manager, you can prepare your employees ahead of time by talking about what reactions they can expect. You could reproduce articles on the subject as a guideline for a change meeting. Encourage people to ask questions and share their feelings. Some managers share their own feelings and personal resistance (this may or may not be appropriate for you). Letting people know that they are not alone, that others have similar reactions and feelings, can help validate their experience and make the phase pass faster.

People need a way to say good-bye to the old ways so that they can begin to welcome the new. One way to help your employees through this bumpy time is by using simple rituals that publicly acknowledge the losses people are experiencing. For example, you might suggest assembling a time capsule with old memos, reports, and so on, to be buried with proper eulogies and an exchange of stories about the past.

RESISTANCE (Continued)

A more elaborate ritual is described in Rosabeth Moss Kantor's recent book, *When Giants Learn to Dance*. She describes an event developed for Western Airlines when the company was acquired by Delta:

> Each of the eight managers attending was asked to write down the three worst things that could happen to them personally as a result of the merger. Then the managers were given sheets of their former letterhead and business cards. The group was led outside and assembled around a wooden casket. A band played a funeral march. One by one, the managers were asked to crumple up their statements, cards, and letterheads and toss them in the coffin. Suddenly, a hundred-ton paver emerged from around the corner. As it approached the coffin, the band broke into a rendition of ''On Wisconsin,'' and the group cheered wildly as the paver flattened the coffin and its contents. Next, the group was whisked back inside where they were given academic caps and gowns to put on. They marched into an auditorium. There the boss gave them a graduation speech and presented each person with a ''Doctorate in Merger Management'' degree and a share of company stock as a graduation gift.

Diagnosing Resistance

You will see anger; blame; anxiety; depression; resentment; work will slow; and people's attitudes will reflect a feeling of ''what's the difference, this company doesn't care any more.''

Managing Resistance

Listen, acknowledge feelings, respond empathetically, encourage support. Accept people's negative responses as appropriate for this phase. Understand that, as difficult as it seems, this phase will pass with time. Help people say good-bye to the old structure by acknowledging their feelings of loss through a ritual.

EXPLORATION

During the exploration phase, energy is released as people focus their attention on the future and the external environment once again. You can encourage employees to get excited about the future by offering a positive vision to compensate for the loss.

From a human standpoint, not all restructuring has undesirable results. The survivors of staff cutbacks often find themselves with greater responsibilities and opportunities than before. If management can lead people into drawing on their innate creative energy, employees can find ways to capitalize on the future.

The exploration phase is by nature chaotic. It can also be exhilarating. Managers guide groups through this phase by creating, with their employees, an inspiring vision of where the organization is now heading. They explore where they stand, the results that need to be achieved, and the opportunities that lie ahead. During this transition, managers begin to develop commitment by setting a clear direction and by empowering people to contribute to the new objectives.

Diagnosing Exploration

You will recognize confusion; chaos; energy; lots of new ideas; and a general lack of focus.

Managing Exploration

Conduct brainstorming, visioning, and planning sessions. Discuss values and priorities, and help people see potential opportunities for the organization and for themselves. Create a focus for creative energy by setting short-term goals.

COMMITMENT

The final phase of the cycle is commitment. During this phase, employees become willing to identify themselves solidly with the new structure. The employees now understand the new direction. They are prepared to learn new ways to work together, and they have renegotiated goals and expectations. The values and actions needed to commit to a new phase of productivity are in place. The employees once again care about the organization and its mission. They feel that their work contributions matter—that they are an important part of meeting organizational goals.

Diagnosing Commitment

You will notice employees beginning to work together with a sense of purpose, enthusiasm, and cooperation; people begin to identify with the organization's mission; and they begin looking for new challenges.

Managing Commitment

Set long-term goals. Concentrate on team building and developing creative problem-solving skills in your employees. Increase group involvement by using quality circles, task forces, and suggestion systems. Validate and reward those responding to the change. Look ahead. Enjoy it!

P A R T

V

The Values-Driven Manager

As time goes by, talking about values will be regarded as absolutely essential—just as essential as marketing or logistics or strategic planning or thinking or decision making.
—Richard Zimmerman, Chairman and
CEO of Hershey Food Corporation

THE NEW ORGANIZATIONAL LOYALTY

Loyalty has two dimensions: an internal or emotional component and an external or behavioral aspect.* Internally, loyalty results in feelings of caring, commitment, and bonding. Externally, loyalty can be manifested in a variety of ways.

LOYALTY

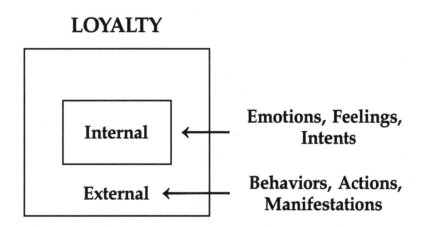

We have witnessed vast changes in workplace loyalty over the past two decades—primarily in the external ways in which management and employees demonstrate commitment.

While companies may no longer guarantee graduation-to-retirement employment, today's management can do many things to demonstrate that they care about their employees' well-being. This section of the book will help you develop those practices.

Today's employees speak of the importance of loyalty at work. They place a high value on reciprocal commitment to an organization that inspires and appreciates their loyalty. They may not choose to manifest this loyalty by staying in one company (or even in one career) forever; but while they are employed, they demonstrate concern for the organization in many ways, some of which we have already examined.

*This section has been adapted from the author's latest book, *The Loyalty Factor: Building Trust in Today's Workplace.* For order information, please contact Kinsey Consulting Services at (415) 943-7850.

NEW ORGANIZATIONAL LOYALTY
(Continued)

It is important to separate the emotions of loyalty (the internal intent) from the actions (the external manifestation). This allows behaviors to change as organizations and people change without destroying genuine caring and commitment.

Here is an interesting set of questions to ask yourself and your team at one of your next meetings. Write your answers in the spaces provided.

1. What manifestations of organizational loyalty would realistically be expected 10 or 20 years ago?

   _____

   _____

   _____

2. What manifestations of employee loyalty could realistically be expected 10 or 20 years ago?

   _____

   _____

   _____

3. What can employees realistically expect from organizations today?

   _____

   _____

   _____

4. What can organizations realistically expect from employees today?

   _____

   _____

   _____

5. What do employees today most need from management that will help build loyalty?

   _____

   _____

   _____

A key word here is *realistic*. Try to focus as much as possible on what is practical and possible in today's business environment.

Research shows that employees' needs are in line with the kinds of practices that the most effective managers already do. Honest communication, ethical dealings, employee participation, appreciation, and respectful treatment may already be a familiar part of your management approach.

A word of caution. Although we are discussing management skills and techniques, remember that the basis of managing for commitment and loyalty lies in your intent. If you genuinely care about your employees, it will be apparent in all your interactions. If you don't have an emotional attachment to your team, all the technique in the world won't be sufficient.

THE SIX STEPS

To gain the commitment of your work group, you must become the kind of manager who commands—rather than demands—respect and trust. Employees become committed when they are treated as part of the team—when they know that their contributions are important. When employees feel understood, considered, and appreciated, their commitment and loyalty grow. These are the six management steps that lead to loyal and committed employees:

Step One: **Communicate Candidly.**

Step Two: **Empower Employees.**

Step Three: **Develop Employees Professionally and Personally.**

Step Four: **Show Appreciation.**

Step Five: **Manage Ethically and Impartially.**

Step Six: **Promote Workplace Wellness.**

The following pages dissect these six steps in detail. Use the questionnaires to evaluate how you currently apply these steps. Identify where you stand now and what improvements you need to make.

STEP ONE: *COMMUNICATE CANDIDLY*

How candidly do you communicate? Rate each statement below according to this scale:

> **4** Almost always true
> **3** True most of the time
> **2** Seldom true
> **1** Almost never true

____ I communicate honestly.

____ My verbal communications are congruent with my actions. I "walk my talk."

____ I admit my mistakes and imperfections.

____ When I am wrong, I apologize.

____ I listen well.

____ I only make promises I can keep.

____ I conduct formal employee interviews.

____ I am candid with prospective employees about the company culture and the job description.

____ I keep my subordinates informed of what is going on in the department and the company.

____ I encourage healthy communication and discourage bickering.

____ I initiate one-on-one contact with all my employees.

____ I maintain my sense of humor and fun when communicating with employees.

____ **TOTAL SCORE**

Evaluation:

Here's what your score indicates:

41 and above: You are a candid communicator.

31-40: Your communication is generally candid, with some exceptions.

21-30: You could be more candid with your employees. It's worth the effort!

Below 20: You're not a very candid communicator. This is a good time to work on being more candid.

STEP TWO: *EMPOWER EMPLOYEES*

Are you good at empowering employees? Assess yourself by rating each statement below according to this scale:

> **4** Almost always true
> **3** True most of the time
> **2** Seldom true
> **1** Almost never true

_____ I delegate well and have faith in an employee's ability to handle the delegated task.

_____ I encourage employees to challenge the status quo.

_____ I keep track of and acknowledge employees' creative ideas and contributions.

_____ I actively seek employee involvement.

_____ I schedule regular meetings for employees to brainstorm without a manager.

_____ I set ''thing agendas''—for example, a problem of the week.

_____ I assign employees to be ''boss'' or ''expert'' for a day.

_____ I consistently ask employees for their responses to proposed company changes.

_____ I work with subordinates to establish mutually agreed-upon goals and strategies for getting the job done.

_____ I allow subordinates to make mistakes.

_____ I support group activity and peer counseling for problem solving and generating ideas.

_____ I allow subordinates to structure their work in ways that are comfortable and productive for them.

_____ **TOTAL SCORE**

Evaluation:

Here's what your score indicates:

41 and above: You understand how to empower your employees.

31–40: You generally do a good job of empowering employees but miss some opportunities for empowerment.

21–30: You could empower your employees much more than you do. Try taking a more empowering approach. The results may surprise you.

Below 20: There's room for a lot of improvement in your empowerment skills. Start working on them today!

STEP THREE: *DEVELOP EMPLOYEES PROFESSIONALLY AND PERSONALLY*

How much do you contribute to employees' development? Rate each statement below according to this scale:

> **4** Almost always true
> **3** True most of the time
> **2** Seldom true
> **1** Almost never true

____ I promote job enrichment and job rotation.

____ I support employee goals, ambitions, and dreams.

____ I provide cross training.

____ I challenge employees to redefine themselves and their work roles.

____ I match employees to potential mentors.

____ I don't let the physical work environment get stale.

____ I ask subordinates what new tasks they would like.

____ I encourage employees to pursue their education goals.

____ I encourage employees to join company committees.

____ I care about my employees' personal problems and offer my assistance and support.

____ I publicize the accomplishments of talented employees.

____ I help people to maximize their strengths and minimize their weaknesses.

____ **TOTAL SCORE**

Evaluation:

Here's the interpretation of your score:

41 and above: You are making an excellent contribution to your employees' professional and personal development.

31-40: You generally make a worthwhile contribution to your employees' development. Look for ways you can contribute even more.

21-30: You could make a much more significant contribution to your employees' development. They'll not only appreciate it—they'll also work better.

Below 20: You're contributing little to your employees' professional and personal development. You can increase your contribution by resolving to change some of the "almost never true" statements to "almost always true."

STEP FOUR: *SHOW APPRECIATION*

Do you show enough appreciation? Or could you learn to show more? Rate each statement below according to this scale:

> **4** Almost always true
> **3** True most of the time
> **2** Seldom true
> **1** Almost never true

_____ I always offer positive reinforcement.

_____ I give verbal encouragement.

_____ I use visual reinforcement, such as thank-you notes and ''employee of the month'' awards.

_____ My appreciation is genuine.

_____ I acknowledge group success.

_____ I acknowledge individual success—both continuing success and improvements.

_____ I stress an individual's potential rather than past problems.

_____ I acknowledge that my major role is to support and facilitate my subordinates.

_____ I give high visibility and a title (lead worker in charge of...) to an employee who accepts a new responsibility or job.

_____ I find creative ways to show appreciation to *all* my subordinates—not just the stars.

_____ I am specific in my praise and appreciation.

_____ When appropriate, I show appreciation to my boss.

_____ **TOTAL SCORE**

Evaluation:

Here's what your score indicates:

4l and above: You are very successful at showing appreciation.

31–40: You often show appreciation (but sometimes you could show a little more).

21–30: You show some appreciation. You can learn to show even more—read through the Step Four statements again.

Below 20: You don't show much appreciation. You probably feel more than you show—why not work on expressing it more successfully?

STEP FIVE: *MANAGE ETHICALLY AND IMPARTIALLY*

Do you have the highest possible standard of ethical and impartial behavior? Rate each statement below according to this scale:

> 4 Almost always true
> 3 True most of the time
> 2 Seldom true
> 1 Almost never true

_____ I am fair with my employees.

_____ I am ethical in my dealings with employees.

_____ I try to be impartial and to avoid favoritism.

_____ I believe that my employees are fair and ethical with me.

_____ I point out ways in which the company is supportive of employee interests.

_____ I believe that my employees are loyal to the company.

_____ I stress consistency in managing employees.

_____ I want my workers to be successful.

_____ I try to see things from the perspective of my employees.

_____ My subordinates' well-being is a part of every one of my management decisions.

_____ I let my employees know what I expect from them in the way of loyalty.

_____ I trust the people who work for me.

_____ **TOTAL SCORE**

Evaluation:

Here's what your score indicates about how you put your ethics into practice:

41 and above: You keep up a high standard of fair and ethical behavior.

31-40: You are generally fair and ethical, with only a few lapses.

21-30: You are not always fair or impartial. It's worth striving to improve this aspect of your management skills and attitudes.

Below 20: Your ethics and impartiality are at a low level. Start working on them today—you'll have a happier workplace as soon as you do.

64

STEP SIX: *PROMOTE WORKPLACE WELLNESS*

To assess how well you promote workplace wellness,* rate each statement below according to this scale:

> **4** Almost always true
> **3** True most of the time
> **2** Seldom true
> **1** Almost never true

____ I encourage employees to attend company-sponsored wellness and health programs.

____ I create a positive work environment.

____ I spread the word about health issues through newsletters or bulletin-board announcements.

____ I bring in vendors and consultants who present wellness programs.

____ I urge subordinates to pursue healthful outside interests.

____ I make healthy food choices available at meetings.

____ I am aware of stress-producing situations at work and do my best to alleviate them.

____ I encourage workers to create and maintain a physically safe work environment.

____ I promote employee fitness by encouraging exercise or stretch breaks during the work day.

____ I am developing a library of books, periodicals, and videos on wellness for employees to use.

____ I publicize community health programs.

____ I give awards to employees who make significant changes in their health behavior.

____ **TOTAL SCORE**

Evaluation:

Here's the interpretation of your workplace wellness score:

41 and above: You do an excellent job of promoting wellness in the workplace.

31-40: You have gone a long way toward workplace wellness. You could go a bit further, though.

21-30: You are doing something to promote wellness, but there's much more that you could be doing.

Below 20: Your efforts to promote wellness in the workplace are almost nonexistent. Consider paying more attention to this sometimes overlooked responsibility of management.

SUMMARY OF THE SIX STEPS

Step One—Communicate candidly

Candid communication means giving timely and reliable information in all your interactions with employees. They especially need to know where the organization is heading, what the company stands for, and how their jobs contribute to the success of the overall operation. When you communicate candidly with employees, you show that you respect them as professionals and as people and they will more readily commit to the goals of the organization.

Step Two—Empower employees

When you give people a measure of control over their work—ask their opinions, listen to their ideas, and get them involved in projects early on—they become more committed. By including employees in the problem-solving process, you meet their need to make creative contributions, and you help insure the success of the company.

Step Three—Develop employees professionally and personally

When you encourage people to grow and develop their potential, they become more committed to the company and more excited about future opportunities. By helping people link their own aspirations to the goals of the organization, you build strong, mutually reinforcing sets of loyalties. When you take an interest in your employees as individuals, you become sincerely and personally involved with them, and you will create a powerful bond of reciprocal trust.

Step Four—Show appreciation

When you give employees approval, praise, and recognition, they respond by becoming more cooperative and committed. According to a long-term psychological study from the University of Michigan, people not only stay around for additional attention, they change and grow in order to receive even more approval.

Step Five—Manage ethically and impartially

"In a general sense," Dr. Albert Schweitzer said, "ethics is the name we give our concern for good behavior. We feel an obligation to consider not only our own personal well-being, but that of others and of human society as a whole." When your interactions with team members are ethical and impartial, you show people that you care about them. Employees are proud to be affiliated with an organization that shows ethical consideration for them and for society. They are inspired to bond and commit to such an organization.

Step Six—Promote workplace wellness

When you participate in health promotion, you are taking care of your most valuable resource: your employees. People are increasingly concerned about their health and wellness. For most of today's workers, health and fitness are top priorities. By acknowledging the importance of these objectives and responding to them by developing organizational wellness programs, you validate the employees' value to the organization. Employees who feel valued by their employers are most likely to reciprocate by increased loyalty and commitment.

P A R T

VI

Commitment
Action Plan

The life of wisdom must be a life of contemplation combined with action.

—M. Scott Peck, *The Road Less Traveled*

CREATE AN ACTION PLAN

It's now time to put together all that you have learned and create an action plan for developing and maintaining commitment in your work force. Following are some questions to help you. Write your answers in the spaces provided.

1. What are the benefits of building commitment to you, your employees, and your organization?

   You _____

   _____

   _____

   Your employees _____

   _____

   _____

   Your organization _____

   _____

   _____

2. How do you develop employee commitment?

   _____

   _____

   _____

   _____

3. List your action steps for each of these six areas:

   Communication _____

   _____

   _____

   _____

ACTION PLAN (Continued)

Empowerment _____
_____
_____
_____

Appreciation _____
_____
_____

Employee development _____
_____
_____
_____

Fairness and ethics _____
_____
_____

Workplace wellness _____
_____
_____
_____

4. What skills, knowledge, and attitudes do you need to develop in order to better manage for commitment?

Skills _____
_____
_____

Knowledge _____
_____
_____

Attitudes _____

_____

_____

5. What are the most important loyalties in your life?

_____

_____

_____

6. How can multiple loyalties in your life better support one another?

_____

_____

_____

7. How does your organization expect employees to show their commitment?

_____

_____

_____

8. How do you expect employees to show their commitment?

_____

_____

_____

9. How do employees expect the organization to show loyalty to them?

_____

_____

_____

ACTION PLAN (Continued)

10. How do employees expect you to show loyalty to them?

_____

_____

_____

11. How can you make sure that these mutual expectations are realistic?

_____

_____

_____

12. What is one concrete action that you can take in the next 30 days that will build more trust and commitment with your employees?

_____

_____

_____

NOTES

FOR OTHER FIFTY-MINUTE SELF-STUDY BOOKS
SEE THE BACK OF THIS BOOK.

NOTES

FOR OTHER FIFTY-MINUTE SELF-STUDY BOOKS
SEE THE BACK OF THIS BOOK.

NOTES

FOR OTHER FIFTY-MINUTE SELF-STUDY BOOKS
SEE THE BACK OF THIS BOOK.

NOTES

FOR OTHER FIFTY-MINUTE SELF-STUDY BOOKS
SEE THE BACK OF THIS BOOK.

$$\boxed{\textbf{NOTES}}$$

NOTES

FOR OTHER FIFTY-MINUTE SELF-STUDY BOOKS
SEE THE BACK OF THIS BOOK.

ABOUT THE FIFTY-MINUTE SERIES

We hope you enjoyed this book and found it valuable. If so, we have good news for you. This title is part of the best selling *FIFTY-MINUTE Series* of books. All other books are similar in size and identical in price. Several books are supported with a training video. These are identified by the symbol **V** next to the title.

Since the first *FIFTY-MINUTE* book appeared in 1986, more than five million copies have been sold worldwide. Each book was developed with the reader in mind. The result is a concise, high quality module written in a positive, readable self-study format.

FIFTY-MINUTE Books and Videos are available from your distributor or from Crisp Publications, Inc., 95 First Street, Los Altos, CA 94022. A free current catalog is available on request.

The complete list of *FIFTY-MINUTE Series* Books and Videos are listed on the following pages and organized by general subject area.

MANAGEMENT TRAINING (Cont.)

PERSONNEL/HUMAN RESOURCES

COMMUNICATIONS

To order books/videos from the FIFTY-MINUTE Series, please:

1. **CONTACT YOUR DISTRIBUTOR**

   or

2. **Write to Crisp Publications, Inc.**
   95 First Street   (415) 949-4888 - phone
   Los Altos, CA 94022   (415) 949-1610 - FAX